Geometric Allover Patterns

Ian O. Angell

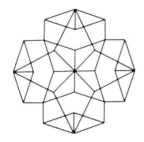

Dover Publications, Inc., New York

INTRODUCTION

Dr. Angell is a senior lecturer in computer science at University College London, England. One of his many research interests is the study and mathematical analysis of geometrical patterns from ancient cultures. In order to illustrate lectures and articles on the art of the Graeco-Roman, Celtic and Islamic cultures, Dr. Angell has generated a series of computer programs, in the Fortran IV computer language, to draw idealized patterns.

The designs given in this book are an unusual by-product of his research. They were produced by the computer program that generates the so-called lattice patterns. These lattice patterns are highly structured and demonstrate various types of repetition and symmetry. The potentially infinite number of lattice patterns fall into 17 categories, each type corresponding to one of the 17 two-dimensional space groups. This fundamental mathematical structure has meant that this kind of geometrical design was developed independently at different times in many cultures throughout the world.

To draw a lattice pattern the computer has first to generate a "tile"; the computer takes an elementary set of line segments and arcs, and manipulates them using a space group (a sequence of reflections, rotations and translations on the original set) into a tile, which introduces some initial symmetry. These tiles are then stacked in a regular lattice in two-dimensional space, thus initiating further symmetries. Such a design is necessarily infinite so Clipping, a technique from computer graphics, is used to restrict the pattern to within a finite rectangle.

A surprising feature of this method of generating what Dr. Angell calls "serendipity patterns" is that even an apparently random, nonsymmetric basic set of lines and arcs can produce beautifully symmetric designs. In addition to the numerous possible artistic applications of the artwork, an interesting pastime might be to work out the tile for each pattern and then find which lines and arcs form that tile by combining reflections, rotations and translations.

Copyright © 1985 by Dover Publications, Inc.
All rights reserved under Pan American and International Copyright Conventions.

Published in Canada by General Publishing Company, Ltd., 30 Lesmill Road, Don Mills, Toronto, Ontario.
Published in the United Kingdom by Constable and Company, Ltd.

Geometric Allover Patterns is a new work, first published by Dover Publications, Inc., in 1985 under the title *Computer Geometric Art*.

DOVER *Pictorial Archive* SERIES

Manufactured in the United States of America
Dover Publications, Inc., 31 East 2nd Street, Mineola, N.Y. 11501

Library of Congress Cataloging in Publication Data

Angell, Ian O.
  Computer geometric art.

  1. Computer graphics.   2. Computer art.   I. Title.
T385.A52   1985   760   84-21181
ISBN 0-486-24855-0

1

3

9

14

16

20

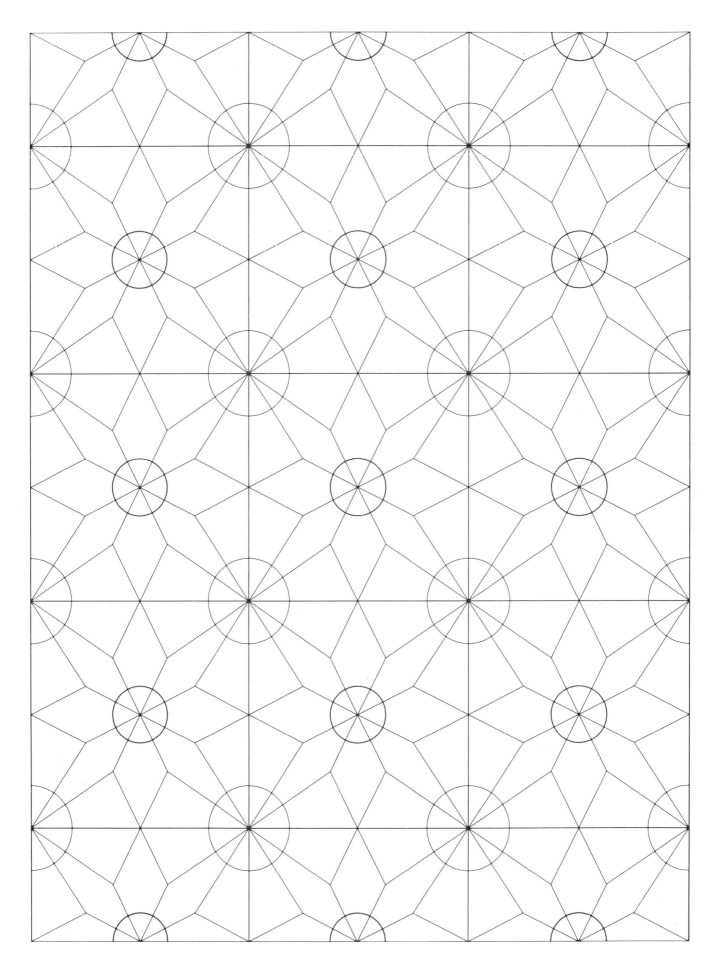

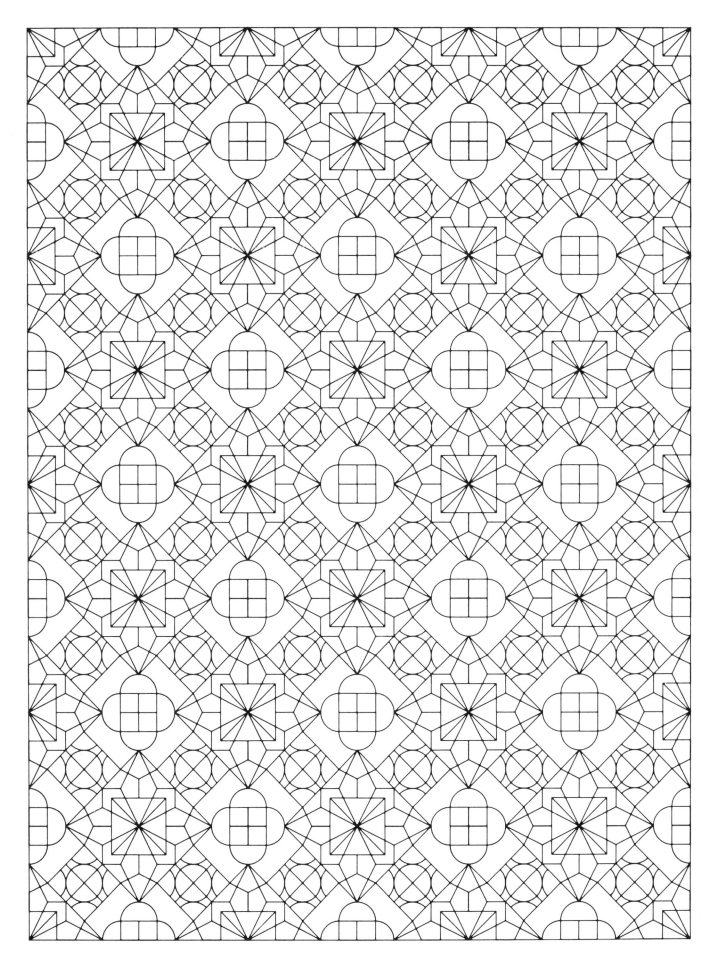

44